How NOT to be a
Ghost Hunter

How NOT to be a Ghost Hunter

Shannon Bradley Byers

Paranormal Genealogist Publishing

2017

First Printing: 2017

ISBN: 978-1-365-58562-3

Paranormal Genealogist Publishing
Lilburn, Georgia
www.paranormalgenealogist.com
www.timelessparanormal.com

For my husband David, whose encouragement, patience and love is infinite, and Jay Dobbertin, who does his best from the other side of the veil to keep me on the right path.

ACKNOWLEDGEMENTS

Over the course of my paranormal "career," I have had support and encouragement from many people. I have also had many thought provoking debates for which I am eternally grateful. The following people have contributed in ways to this book that only they will understand and even if you thought I wasn't listening, I was: Dale Epley, Laura Larmore, Trena Evans, Pam Brooks, William Aymerich, Jeffrey Lewis, Richard Estep, Kenny Biddle, Tim Woolworth, Michael Morgan, Dawn Jones, Amber Truax, Joel Sturgis, and my Black Knight in VERY shiny armor wielding a mighty red pen, Mark Baron.

It goes without saying, but I will say it anyway, that my mother, Stephanie Bradley, had a heck of a lot to do with helping me accomplish my dream of becoming an author. Not only did she do the first edit on this book, but she is also the one that fostered my drive and passion for research. She taught me the importance of validating my research even if, that passion gave her more work to do. She always makes time to help me, even if it is something she is not really interested in. Love you Mama!

A special thanks has to be given to Kyl T. Cobb, Jr. Not only do I consider him a friend, I consider him a researcher of the highest caliber. Kyl is the first person I've met in this field who takes research as seriously as I do. He constantly pushes and advises me when I've run into a brick wall and reminds me to do things I've momentarily forgotten I can do. His friendship, guidance, and editing advice mean the world to me and this would not be a published work if it were not for him.

Table of Contents

Introduction

When I was eight years old, I saw a book at a school book fair titled "Haunted Houses" by Larry Kettelkamp. The picture on the cover ignited in me a lifelong passion of capturing evidence of a ghost.

Around the same time, a series appeared on television called "In Search of..." Every week Leonard Nimoy would tell me about people looking for aliens, Bigfoot, the Loch Ness monster, ancient mysteries, and of course my favorite, ghosts. He, and occasionally Hans Holzer, would spend 23 minutes with me each week giving me information that served to add gasoline to my paranormal fire. I read every book, fiction and nonfiction, that I could get my hands on to add to my education. I spent my summer vacations taking pictures in centuries old cemeteries and staring out in the distance at battlefields, all in the hopes of seeing manifestations that would give me my own personal experience, and hopefully evidence viewed through the camera lens.

To say I have made mistakes along the way is an understatement and I am not ashamed to share those with you. This book is not meant to be a literary masterpiece, an A to Z guide, or a technical manual. It is simply a way for me to share things with you that I have learned either by experiment, mistake (humiliating or not), or the kindness of those more knowledgeable than I. I want you to learn that you cannot know how to conduct an investigation just by watching television, and to take the programs for what they are: entertainment. Serious paranormal investigators always joke that if cameras were following them around, it would be the most boring TV show ever, but in reality, it is the truth. There have been times I almost fell asleep because it is not always exciting.

I do not claim to have all the answers. I do not know anyone that does, but I have always felt that learning from someone else's experiences is the best schooling you can get. I am sure I left something out that someone will want to ask questions about. If I did, go to my website or find me on Facebook and ask. If I do not know, I will tell you. This book is really about getting you to think, and opening a dialogue between you and me or your own colleagues.

Over the last forty years, I have parked myself at scores of battlefields, cemeteries, and historical locations with my camera and voice recorder in the attempt to capture something I could share that would ignite the same passion in someone else that I found when I was eight.

Cameras have changed a lot since the 1970s but even with the improvements, capturing a ghost on "film" is no easier now than it was then, but with the advent of photo editing software, you can find fakes everywhere. It is interesting to note, though, that faked photos are not new. In the Victorian era, photographers were already managing to manipulate photo plates to show all sorts of ghostly images.

In our current age of "ghost hunting," we have a lot of equipment that touts its ability to get the evidence that so many of us want. Equipment designed for other uses has been incorporated and labeled such things as ghost detector, ghost meter, or ghost finder. Applications for finding ghosts with your cell phone are just a search and a click away. People are relying more and more on "gadgets" because they see them used on TV shows and some never take the time to learn what the real life application for it is.

My husband and I independently started looking for ghosts when we were younger and when we met in 2003 it was only natural that we do it together. Countless hours were spent in pursuit of our childhood dreams and moments were never wasted at historical places, or places we thought felt "spooky." I could not even begin to guess at the number of digital photos we have taken together in the last 13 years, and yet in all that time we have only caught something one time that we cannot explain.

I tried for many years to get on a ghost hunting team. I was sure that my years spent as a historical and family researcher would be an asset, since I had been doing that since the age of 13. I am very good at tracking down information. My research has been featured in many published works by other authors, and I have been called upon by historical societies and owners of historic locations to fill in their gaps.

In 2013, we did find a startup team that was willing to have David and me, but it did not last long. We quickly learned about the drama that is so prevalent in paranormal teams. So we parted ways and decided that there really was no need for doing it with other people. We would just keep doing what we had been doing on together for 10 years.

One frustrating obstacle we encountered was while trying to get permission to investigate historical locations. Since so many "ghost hunting" teams had gone to locations and behaved less than honorably, the people in charge wanted resumes and references, which we did not have. In August of 2013, we decided to organize, come up with a clever name, and get our black t-shirts! It took me weeks to find a name that was not in use; even the most obscure ones I could think of were gone. One night the name finally came to me, and Timeless Paranormal was born. I decided on Timeless to honor those spirits that were oblivious to time. I spent countless hours writing letters and making phone calls to get our name out there.

I wanted something special to add to my social media posts, so I ran a feature on our website called Timeless Tuesday. Each week I would highlight a newspaper article about ghosts written in the 1700s, 1800s, and early 1900s. These articles were eye opening and proved how long and earnestly people have been trying to prove the existence of ghosts. If you read any of the articles, you will also see that faking evidence was as prevalent back then as it is now, only now, with the advancement of technology, it is far easier.

We set about finding residential and business clients that needed help, and we quickly had a list of references that we could provide to others, and the doors that have magically opened to us have provided some of the most amazing experiences we have ever had, together or apart. We have also learned firsthand what doors "ghost hunters" have closed because of their behaviors. It did not hurt that my best friend, Laura, was on the historical commission for a historic property in south Georgia and they not only allowed us to investigate there, they invited us to their county fair and promoted us whenever they could. This eventually led to being able to investigate state parks and super-secret locations that changed our lives in ways that it would take a different book to explain. Their faith and trust in us catapulted us into the paranormal mainstream and we were soon taking on cases in other states.

Social media can be a tricky thing, and unfortunately I fell into the whole "para unity" trap for a while before I learned it was just an excuse for bad behavior in some. The concept of para unity was a good one; the paranormal community coming together as one and working for a common cause. Unfortunately, in many cases if you show that another team is faking evidence, providing false evidence (such as orbs) you are accused of being a bully. There are literally thousands of "ghost hunting" teams out there. Each of us is involved for our own reasons. Each of us have our own set of beliefs on what is and is not evidence. Each of us has developed our own investigation dos and don'ts. David and I are no different in that.

We are a husband and wife team that have been together for over thirteen years and we love going to a location to collect data using various investigatory strategies to try to prove what has been rejected by science. We understand that in a world saturated with books, websites, and television shows, it is hard to separate what COULD be normal every day occurrences from the "unexplained." Unfortunately, too many people feel that manufacturing results will get them wherever it is they want to be in this "profession."

We do this because we want to help people understand what could be going on around them, and that not every knock in the wall or object that falls over is demonic activity. We are not out to be on television. We have been contacted several times to do TV shows, and when we made it extremely clear that we would not do one single thing that was not honest and aboveboard, we were dismissed and that is ok with us.

Do we have beliefs that do not agree with other groups? Of course we do. Do we use investigation techniques that other peers may not agree with? Of course we do. Is that ok with us? Of course it is. No two groups are ever going to be the same when it comes to everything involved with paranormal research, because there are just too many variables and belief systems.

We like to have fun; we really enjoy the historical places we get to go and the people we get to meet along the way, but we are serious about what we do. We approach every investigation as skeptics, meaning that while we personally believe in ghosts, we do not believe every location we go to is haunted. We understand that a person who might have had a true paranormal experience may start to see everything happening around them as paranormal. They may not always understand or they lose sight of real world situations that could cause what they are experiencing.

We take the claims of occurrences and always try to find the "normal" explanation first. We are firm believers that not everything is paranormal and that a large percentage of things CAN be explained very simply. If you are looking for someone that thinks every "orb" or "mist" or "light anomaly" is a spirit, we are not the team for you. We have spent years learning what our cameras will produce in various situations, and we are well versed in ghost apps. We will not accept any case where they are presented to convince us there is activity in your location. The worst thing we could do is waste either your time or ours if we do not think we can help you.

To a majority of people the terms "ghost hunter" and "paranormal investigator/researcher" are interchangeable. Most of the time when you tell a person you are a paranormal investigator, they look kind of blank until you say "I'm a ghost hunter" and the light bulb appears above their head and they say "oh cool!"

These days, there is a quickly growing number of us that find the term "ghost hunter" offensive. The term no longer denotes the level of seriousness that we strive for in what we do.

In 2004 when the TV show, Ghost Hunters, first aired, those of us in the field were excited. Our passion was finally being broadcast to the mainstream. Little did we know what a double-edged sword it was going to turn into. The term "ghost hunter" is not going to go away. It is too deeply imbedded in everyone's mind. Heck, even our chief of police introduces us to everyone as his "favorite ghost hunters." Next time you use the term, please remember that there are a lot of us that no longer want to be referred to that way and it is my hope that when you reach the end of this book, you will understand the difference.

There are currently about 17 paranormal shows still airing new episodes (in the US). More than double that number are still airing in reruns and at least three new shows in current development. Unfortunately, instead of highlighting what we take seriously, some of them have turned into something of a joke and made millions of people around the world think they can be instant ghost hunters. They believe they can run to the closest internet "ghost hunting equipment store," buy a lot of gadgets, take them somewhere and know what they are doing because they saw it on TV all in the name of fun. All they are doing is putting themselves and others into potentially dangerous situations.

David and I have been guests at conventions like Dragon Con & ScareFest; we give monthly historical tours and talks about what we do and they are usually well received. The first time we were asked to speak at Dragon Con, I was terrified I was going to be put with people that thought differently than we did and I wondered how the panels would go. In the past, I had been asked to help several other teams and was dismayed at their thought processes and investigation procedures. I was pleasantly surprised when we sat down with the members of Paranormal Georgia Investigations to brainstorm our discussions and found out they thought the same way we did. The discussions I have had with their members since then have been valuable to my knowledge base and we consider them not only colleagues, but also friends.

"How NOT to be a Ghost Hunter" is a concept born of the frustration felt by my good friend William Aymerich and me. Will has been kind enough to have me on his radio show many times, and we have spent a lot of time talking about this frustration. We finally decided we wanted to teach a class that showed investigators what they might be missing or simply did not know, in order to provide better tools to use than the ones they had gotten from watching TV. The first seminar we had was twelve people of varying backgrounds. Some of them were not even investigators; they were just interested in what we do.

In 2016, ScareFest asked me to condense the 4-hour class into a 45-minute seminar, which was no easy feat. The feedback we got from the presentation and others that had read an early copy of the class manual was great. I received several suggestions that I put it in book form to make it widely available to those that were interested and could not make it to Atlanta for a class, or to a convention that included all things paranormal.

Which brings us here, to this book. Before you get your first piece of equipment, come up with a catchy name, or buy your t-shirts, the first thing you need to ask yourself is "why do I want to do this?" The answer to this question will determine many things. If it is just for thrill seeking, you might want to rethink your decision. As in all things, thrill seeking can have detrimental effects on yourself and others.

Can you think of three reasons that you want to be a paranormal investigator/researcher? Make a note of those in your head right now. I hope that when you are finished reading, those reason will be clearer for you.

Those That Came Before Us

When I worked on the Timeless Tuesday feature, I always enjoyed the headlines of the articles I dug up. Some of them were serious, some were condemning, and others were just silly. The articles themselves proved the adage "there is nothing new under the sun." Those of us interested in the pursuit of the paranormal are asking the same questions people were asking centuries ago.

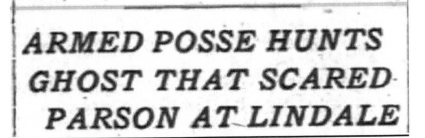

Atlanta Constitution 1914

Chicago Tribune 1907

Chicago Tribune 1902

Ghost Hunter Gets Good Pay;
How Would You Like the Job?
By B. M. Hall.

Chicago Tribune 1906

Present Status of the Ghost

SPOOKS COMING INTO THEIR OWN SINCE SCIENCE HAS BE-
GUN TO INVESTIGATE THEM

Washington Post 1912

Chicago Tribune 1900

11

Fort Wayne News 1900

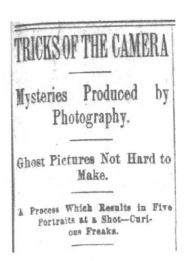

San Francisco Chronicle 1893

GHOST-LAYING THE LATEST OF LONDON'S PROFESSIONS

HEADQUARTERS OF THE GHOST LAYERS.
Charles Dove, the Organizer of the Spook Exterminators, Is Shown in the Doorway.

Atlanta Constitution 1908

A Team in the Making

I cannot stress a few things enough; one of them is that no one should EVER investigate alone. There are far too many dangers, seen and unseen, that you can encounter. Always work with at least one other person.

When you are choosing the people you want to do this with there are several things that you want to keep in mind, and it might not be what you are thinking.

Yes, your team needs to be on the same page as far as ethics and safety go, but you do not all have to think alike. Including a skeptic on your team can be very beneficial, because in the heat of the moment your rational mind can become irrational in the blink of an eye. Having someone that can keep the team grounded is a good thing, as long as they are respectful. You, yourself, may not believe in mediums or dead seers, but having a sensitive or medium that you can use as a tool can be beneficial in testing ideas; just do not rely on them for ALL of your investigation.

You will need someone that is good at and enjoys research. You will need someone that has a good eye for detail and you will need someone that is not averse to the mind numbing hours required for evidence review. If you can do all that with two people great. David and I have done that for years with no problems. There is no rule that says you have to have a 15-person team (and often times there are huge drawbacks to big teams). You need a tech guru so that when you decide what equipment you are going to use, you have someone that knows how to learn to use it properly. Some questions you should ask: what is the real life application it was made for? How is it supposed to benefit an investigation?

Just knowing something can read electromagnetic fields (EMF) does not really tell you a whole lot if you do not understand what EMF is or why you should be looking for it. What are the differences in the types of cameras? Why is using a cell phone camera a bad idea? Why is using a cell phone at all a bad idea? Do you know what the theory behind a spirit box is and how it is supposed to work?

Do you know enough about the way a camera works to understand why the pictures might show orbs, trails, supposed apparitions, or ectoplasm? Do you know what things investigators used before items specifically marketed for the paranormal came on the marketplace? Do you know what your single most important piece of equipment is?

What will your moral and ethics code be? What rules will you have for your team members? What will the result of breaking those rules be? How will you share this with your potential clients? How will you attempt to prove to your clients that you are trustworthy? Do you have a backup plan if the member with the thermal camera quits and takes it with them? Do you have a trustworthy person to handle the funds you have all pooled together to fund trips and equipment purchases?

How will you systematically go about debunking, (proving that it is not paranormal), a client's claims? Will you be able to handle a client that insists you are wrong and that there IS a demon in the house, no matter how you can positively show them it is knocking from the water pipes?

How will you protect yourself from a potentially dangerous client? How will you protect yourself from safety hazards? Do you know that there is no "rule" that says you MUST investigate at night? Do you know why it is beneficial NOT to kick out your clients during the investigation?

If all of these questions have not scared you off, do not get comfortable, there are more questions to come as we dig a little deeper into the ideologies and techniques required to transition from "ghost hunter" to paranormal investigator.

The Client Interview

Congratulations, you have been contacted by a potential client for help! What now? Fact gathering, of course. A few different kinds of contact can and should take place before any investigating happens.

Initial Contact

This can happen in various ways: a phone call, an email, a message on Facebook, a conversation at a party (when your helpful friend introduces you as a ghost hunter) etc.

Once upon a time, there was an embarrassing afternoon at our home when David and I were getting ready to attend the opera that evening. I had just gotten out of the shower and David had gotten in when the doorbell rang. I was wrapped up in a body towel with my head swathed in a turban when I saw through the window that it was the local police. It was not just a regular patrol officer either, oh no, it was one of the sergeants! Since we work closely with our local law enforcement, I was afraid something had happened and I had no choice but to answer the door. I was standing there, completely mortified when I found out he had stopped by to give me the business card of a nearby funeral home because the manager wanted to talk to us about some things that were going on there. Did I mention I was mortified?

No matter how they contact you (hopefully you are dressed), the first steps are pretty basic. You ask what is happening and most importantly, why they believe it is paranormal. The second part of that question is important because it not only gives you an idea about the way they think, but it also can show you if you are going to have to combat "ghost hunter TV syndrome."

If this is taking place in a phone call, make sure to take detailed notes. If it is at a party and you have made sure you are both sober, find a piece of paper and a pen to take notes. If you are like me, grab the voice recorder you carry everywhere and ask permission to record the conversation. If the initial contact is via electronic messaging, make sure to keep those conversations so that you can refer back to them later. You will be surprised how much you can tell about a potential client during a voice conversation, so be sure to tell them you need to speak with them personally.

The second thing you need to find out is where they are geographically located. If they are 4 hours away, are you willing to travel on your own dime to do the investigation? Can you afford to potentially take time off work, book a hotel, pay for gas and food? If your budget will not allow that, make sure you have a backup team that you can recommend to the person.

Once you have established that it is a location you can and will go to, you can ask for more detail on what is happening. You will want to know how people at the location are being affected, if it is happening in more than one place in the residence or business and when they notice these things happening. You will find that their recall on some things is good and on others not so much. At this point, you will want to ask them to start writing information down (journaling). Have them write down as much as they remember about past events AND any events that happen prior to your arrival.

Details need to include:
- Date
- Time
- Where
- Who experienced it
- What happened just prior to the event
- What happened during the event
- How did they feel before, during and after the event
- What did they do about the event
- Were they on any medications (OTC or prescription), alcohol or illegal drugs (be prepared for dishonesty on this one, but you still need to ask)

Once they see you are actually going to make them do some work before you do anything, it will help to weed out the ones that just want to say "ghost hunters" came to their house. I have lost count of the hundreds of potential clients that I never heard from again when I explained they had to do this step.

Witness Interview

Once you have gotten as much information as you can, you and your team need to decide if you want to proceed with the investigation. If you do not, let the client know and have a recommendation for another team ready to give them.

If you do, then you need to arrange a time to visit the location to do a more detailed client interview so that you can get all the information you need to begin your research. Many of the questions are the same so it is easier if you have a form, like the one included in the appendix, to use each time. If the location is too far away, you will have to do the in-person client interview immediately before the investigation, so get as much of this detail beforehand as you can. When you conduct the in-person interview, it is best to both video and voice record it, with the client's permission. This will give you two ways to go back, reference it, and give you the opportunity to record any anomalies that may happen. If children are involved, I recommend getting them to draw what they saw so that you can see it from their perspective. It might look like a Picasso, but it will still be helpful.

Pre-Investigation Research

Investigating possible paranormal activity is not just about showing up at a location, turning your gear on, and sitting around in the dark waiting for something to happen. At least it is not to me. I believe that as a paranormal investigator, you have an obligation to your client to know as much about the history of the area as you know about how to run your equipment.

Earthbound spirits, those that have not crossed over, do not have to be attached to a structure as is often evidenced by the ones that decided to follow us home on occasion. Often times you will hear people say, "This house isn't that old, I don't understand why I am experiencing these things." Learning the history of not only the existing structure, structures that stood before, the town, the families that lived there, what happened to them and how to talk to them can possibly get you results you never dreamed of. The history of people currently living there is also important, that is why one of the questions on the questionnaire pertains to activity at their previous homes.

Pre-investigation research can provide you invaluable tools to use during your time at a location. Did the town your location is in suffer some kind of tragedy in its past? Do you know who has owned the land for the last 200 years? Do you know the families that have lived there? Do you know how they died? Do you know how to talk to someone who lived 150 years ago?

I will go through five different kinds of things you can research so that you go into investigation armed with knowledge to help you understand the energy you may encounter and help you communicate better with them.

You cannot always rely on witness history recollections. Unfortunately, sometimes, oral histories that have been passed down are like the game of telephone we used to play as kids. Facts are muddled, changed, attached to the wrong people, and sometimes people just make stuff up to make it sound more fascinating. This is why, along with witness interviews, you need to learn how to conduct research yourself so you can go in with ironclad facts to help you make a good game plan for your investigation.

Town History

Sometimes your work is easy. You know when you go to a location that something bad happened there. Asylums, hospitals, and prisons are good examples of knowing what kind of general history a place will have. Be wary of "legends" though, often times these are embellished or just plain fabricated.

Now, what if it is just a house or business in a nice little town? When you go to a location, do you ever wonder about the town itself? Has the town had different names? Was there anything that caused mass or untimely death? Has any kind of tragedy happened there? Were there any catastrophic weather events (floods, tornadoes, earthquakes, etc.), plane crashes, train wrecks, building explosions, war battles, or mass murders? Did boll weevils wipe out a way of life that might have made someone experience enough mental anguish to go on a rampage? Were gentlemanly duels or high noon showdowns a way of life in this town? Were there torrid love affairs? Was the town struck down by yellow fever, typhoid, or measles? Any one of those scenarios can help you try to figure out what might be going on at your investigation spot.

There are many ways you can find important information about the town you are investigating. This is where the internet and Google WILL be your friend. I know it may be odd to post web links in a book, but most of them will be easy to just type in your browser, and well worth your time to check out.

One of the first things you want to do is search to find out if the town has a local historical society; some do, and some do not. If you cannot find one for the city, search for one for the county/state that town is in. On websites like these, you will be able to find out a lot of basic history. Information can include when the town was formed, why it was formed, if it ever went by another name, if it was ever in another county (this will be beneficial knowledge with the topic of Land Deeds), and if the town is known for anything tragic. Reading through historical websites is an easy, free way to find out some facts, and most of them will give you a contact name that might be willing to help. Be wary of sites that allow users to edit the information that is shared, many times you will find out they have just added unsubstantiated legends.

Word of advice – because of the way some people perceive "ghost hunters", when you need local historians to help, start by telling them you are researching the town and need some assistance. Leave the "paranormal" part out of the conversation until you can gauge whether they are open minded to that type of thing.

Another excellent online source are the county, parish or borough genealogical websites. The US GenWeb project is a decent resource depending on the county administrator who runs it. Some of them have been left to flounder, but some of them have a wealth of information. You can find a state or county listing at http://usgenweb.org. For international information, you can try the website at http://www.worldgenweb.org.

If you live near the town, you can visit the historical society itself and go through real documents that show you the history. Many local libraries have old newspapers on microfilm, and if you found notations of a particular incident, you can go and read the factual stories as they happened. Newspaper accounts written at the time of the incident are gold mines of information that may have been forgotten or changed over time.

A good example of this would be the case of Lavinia Fisher and The Old Charleston Jail. TV shows and tours will tell you (among other things) that while wearing her wedding dress (and a noose), she shouted, "If any of you have a message for the devil, say it now for I shall see him in a moment" and flung herself off the platform before the hangman could perform his duties.

According to the newspaper account at the time, what she actually said was *"Cease, I will have none of it. Save your words for others that want them. But if you have a message you want to send to Hell give it to me; I'll carry it."* When the sheriff assured her no pardon was coming, Lavinia cried out to God in panic and eventually made her peace. She and her husband, John, were driven by cart about a mile away from the jail and hung while wearing traditional hanging clothes; she was not in her wedding dress.

You can also try to find newspaper articles online, the website at https://sites.google.com/site/onlinenewspapersite has many links to historical newspapers, both national and international, that have been digitized and are keyword searchable. One important thing to note when researching old newspaper articles is not limit yourself to just the town. A perfect example occurred when we were planning an investigation in Winder, Georgia. I was looking for an article on the death of a prominent doctor and I could not find it in the local newspaper. Winder sits between Atlanta and Athens, and both newspapers in those towns wrote about the doctor's illness and death. Never limit your research, widen your scope if you have to.

Once you have learned about the area you are going to and the general ways of life in any given time, you can start learning about the specific property and people.

Land Deeds

Land deeds can be a little harder to research, but they can also be SO rewarding. These days local county tax assessor websites can give you some information on the sales of the property back to a certain time, but these times will vary. They generally go back about 30 years or so. The online records can tell you when the structures on the property were built, but keep in mind these dates CAN be incorrect. There have been many times that I have done deed research and found out the date the home was built conflicted with what the homeowner thought it was. It is not uncommon to find out the client thought the home had been built in the1930s, and it turned out the existing structure had been built in 1921. This gives you another approximate 10 years to find families that might have lived there. You do not need to get permission to look for property records; they are public records, but as a show of good faith to the client, you should always tell them you would be looking up these records as part of your research. It is entirely possible that they have already done this research themselves and are willing to share their information, which will save you a LOT of time and headache.

Land deed research has to be done in reverse order, from the present to the past. If the county did have online records, you can use the deed book information listed and go to the county courthouse acquire the names of the grantee and grantor. From there, you systematically use each sale to get the names to search for in the index books until you find the previous sale. Each time you will use that information to do another search, and keep going back as far as you can find records.

Learning the language for the very old deeds can be tricky. The following is an example of a land description, and as you will see, they depended on the fact that trees and rocks would always stay in place:

> *That track or parcel of land situate lying and being in the 243 Dist G.M. said state & county beginning at a black gum at Chandler's line N 21 ½ W 12.50 to a rock N 166 °13.60 to road thence down road S 35 ½ E3 chs. S 52 E 10.34 chs to a rock S 32 E 4.50 chs. to a rock N 78 ½ E 6.47 to a rock thence N 46E 2.80 to*

a post oak. Thence N 73 E 14.00 to a rock at Elder's line. Thence S 35 ½ E 1.5to Iron Wood. Thence East 80 links to white oak thence down the creek 6 chs to white oak the Candler line S 71 W 40.20 to the beginning Black Gum containing 43 acres.

That description is of the lot of land going by all four corners. Links and chs (chains) are a common form of measurement when doing land surveys, if you are interested in the history of a Gunter's Chain, you can read about it at http://www.rushdenheritage.co.uk/land/gunterchain.html.

Yes, this is time consuming, yes, this is frustrating, but it is worth it. Deed recording will vary in countries outside the US so you will have to learn different systems if you do international research.

I mentioned earlier that knowing a town's place in the county is important; it is not rare for a town to have been in multiple counties over the course of its history. We will go back to the Winder, Georgia investigation to illustrate this. The town is currently located in Barrow County, but that is not where it has always been or what it has always been called. Winder was originally a Creek Indian settlement known as Snodon. In 1793, when white men moved in, they named it The Jug; in 1803, it was renamed Jug Tavern. In the 1880s, Jug Tavern was actually located in three different counties: Jackson, Walton, and Gwinnett. In 1894, it was renamed for the last time to Winder and in 1914, a new county was formed to encompass the entire city; they named this county Barrow. If you lost count, that is four different counties for the same town that went by multiple names.

When you are doing research, you need to know what county the property was in at any given time. The land records will be in the courthouse of the county the property was in when it was sold. The online tax records indicated the Winder home had been built in 1887. This meant I had to figure out which of the three counties the lot was in at that time. In this case, it was Jackson. I followed the Jackson county deed books on the property back to the early 1800s, and then I had to go to the existing county, Barrow, and search from 1914 to present day. It was well worth the effort. It showed me that the existing house, which had been a boarding house, funeral home, and private residence, was actually the second house to have been built there. Because I had this information, it helped greatly in locating photographs of the first house that no one seemed to remember had been there.

You never want to limit your investigation to reports about the existing house or business. The more you know about what has been there, the further you can broaden your range of questions when you do electronic voice phenomena (EVP) sessions, and it will give you a greater understanding of responses you might get that seem totally irrelevant.

Genealogy

This topic is one that I could write about incessantly. I have been a genealogist for over 35 years and have spent my life helping other people find out about their family history. Incredibly, it comes in quite handy when conducting paranormal investigations. The more information you can arm yourself with going in, the more the data collected might mean to you. To illustrate this, I will use an example of an investigation we did in our own town for the City Property Development Authority. The home was constructed in 1826 on a 500-acre plantation and it had never officially been investigated. I had wanted to get in there since I was a little girl largely because it had its own cemetery. We had no reports of activity to go on as the last owner of the home died in 1971 and since then had just been a "historic site" that no one lived in.

I systematically developed abbreviated family trees on the last owner, who had lived there for 81 years and died at the age of 97 and the owners before that. Luckily, for me, all the owners had been related since the house had been passed down in the family during various marriages. The original owners had a son named James that fought in the civil war and subsequently died in 1862, but amazingly, was buried in the family cemetery on the property.

This was unusual because he was not a man of rank, and the "norm" was that men were buried where they died, not sent home, unless the family had money to get them home. Everything I could find him mentioned in only said he had "died in South Carolina in service to his country." Everyone assumed he had died in battle. Using the state archives, I got his service record to see what battles he had been in and where he might have actually died. Considering what I had been reading, I was surprised to learn that James developed an unnamed disease and had been sent home where he died in the very house we were going to investigate. That explained how he came to be buried there. Having this information allowed me to do detailed EVP sessions because I had relevant information and was not just taking a "stab in the dark." Because I had not only his service record, but also the records of his unit, which included their movements and their history, I could ask him about his comrades by name and places he had been.

Service records for several wars (along with MANY other useful records) can be found at the National Archives http://www.archives.gov, at one of their many US libraries, or various state archives. There are also online resources, for things like that, like http://www.fold3.com, or http://ancestry.com but these sites cost money in the form of a yearly subscription fee.

Often times, if you have a name, you can do a simple Google search and find free family trees or blogs that family members have put online to include pictures of the people, family stories, etc., that you can use to gather information to ask your questions. A targeted Google search for the area you are investigating can help you locate where those records are, as each country is different in the way they present them and the cost for accessing them. I will not advocate subscriptions for any one particular site, as they are all helpful in their own way. If you are serious about your research, I do recommend finding the one that can give you the most bang for your buck and investing in a yearly subscription to a place that gives you access to a myriad of different kinds of records so that you can learn about your potential interviewee. I know I have used mine just as much for paranormal research as I have for just "regular" genealogy, and the information gathered has been invaluable.

Another great example was the time we had an investigation in a historic home. This was a previous residence turned museum, full of "facts" presented on wall plaques. With due diligence, I not only proved some of their facts incorrect, I found some they had never heard of. A particular resident of that house in the 1860s, Manny, who later died there, was made the flag bearer for the Confederate unit formed in the town. Via a published family genealogy, I found that when he left for the war he did so with the unit flag in one hand and "his fighting cock" in the other. In other words, he left with his prize-fighting rooster so that the men in the unit could engage in cock fighting in between skirmishes and battles. It was not recorded how long the rooster lasted; only that it won many fights. This kind of information is the difference between possibly engaging the spirit there and having them ignore you.

The links I gave previously for http://usgenweb.org and http://www.worldgenweb.org will also be useful for things like this. Many times, you can find family histories written long ago along with copies of bible records. Sometimes these records are the only place you might find the name of someone relevant, especially children that died young and have been lost to time.

Searching http://books.google.com is what supplied me with the information about Manny and his rooster, which will probably go down in history as my favorite pre-investigation fact learned. Researching family histories make the investigation more personal, because when you get to know the possible ghost as a real person that lived and died, I truly believe they can sense your intent and will want to communicate with you.

Life Records

Vital records are a great way of getting information about a person or persons that might have relevance to your location. After a certain time (this is determined by your county, state, or country) you can find copies of birth, death, and marriage records online. Different locations started keeping these records at various times. You might find that one place has marriage records beginning in the 1700s and that another did not officially start keeping them until after 1900 (South Carolina is a good example of this). It is the same for birth and death records.

Depending on the location and type of the record, you can possibly learn where they were born, what they did for a living, who their spouse and parents were, how they died, and where/how they were buried. One thing to keep in mind though is that these records are only as good as the source of information, and that information may not be completely correct.

As stated before, word of mouth stories can be inaccurate. The example I gave of James and how he died of disease instead of gloriously being shot in battle is a good illustration. If death certificates had been issued in 1862, we would know what disease had claimed James. One could surmise it was something extremely contagious and terminal in order to be sent home, but it is something we will probably never know.

Census records are another thing that can help. The census is taken every ten years and records are available from the first one done in 1790 to the 16th one in 1940. Websites vary on whether they charge you to see them, so you can use this link to see who has them and if they charge to view them https://familysearch.org/learn/wiki/en/United_States_Census

These records can give you a glimpse of who lived in the area, what they did for a living, who their children were etc. Sometimes these records can also be invaluable AFTER an investigation. During a particular investigation in Lumpkin, Georgia, we met a 6-year-old little girl ghost named Sarah and through EVP sessions, we gathered some information. This child was not written up in any of the family histories and she was not included in any of the family trees. Using the information we received, I searched census records for the area at the time she indicated she passed, and I found her. The local historical commission was thrilled to be able to add this documented information to their files, and impressed that what the little girl had said in the EVP sessions was proven when no one had any clue she ever existed. It certainly increased their belief in the activity at the location since they were there to witness us receiving the information.

One of my favorite records is something called a Bastardy Bond. These were cause for many a "mysterious disappearance" or outright killing. These bonds were intended to protect the county or other local authority from the cost of raising the child. From the 1700s to the early 1900s, when the pregnancy of an unmarried woman was brought to the attention of the court, a warrant was issued. She was then questioned under oath and asked to name the father of the child. If she named a man, he was served with a warrant and required to post bond. If she refused to name the father, she or her father could post the bond, or else she was arrested and sent to jail. This kind of stuff is fodder for many local towns' urban legends about the deaths of people, and the very thing ghost stories are made of.

Knowing how and where someone died can be beneficial to your investigation, but keep in mind the other information you can get from these records can be useful as well.

Alternate Terminology

Sometimes I like to think of investigation as time travel. If you think about that for a minute, it makes sense. You, yourself, are not actually going anywhere, but you are attempting to communicate with someone from another time. A lot of words and phrases we use now would not be understood 20 years ago, much less 150, 200, or 300 years in the past. Did you know that "way back when" people were classified by different words according to their age? They used designations like baby, little boy/girl, young man/lady, adult man/woman-the word teenager would not be understood until around the 20th century and this is an important thing to keep in mind when attempting to communicate and establish the age of the spirit.

Diseases were known by different names according to the time and geographic location. I did an investigation once where we received an EVP response that the person had died from "spots." Had I not been familiar with alternate terminology, I would not have immediately known that she meant the measles. Do you know that consumption was another term used for someone who had tuberculosis, Grippe was the word for influenza (flu), and Cramp Colic was the term for appendicitis? If you wanted to ask if a person had suffered a stroke, would you use the word "stroke" or would you use "apoplexy"? That would depend on when the person lived. If you are questioning a female who died after giving birth, would you ask if she died from septicemia or childbed fever?

Using the right words will help to get you better responses that you can understand. This website is a good source for locating the kinds of medical terms you should know: http://www.cyndislist.com/medical/diseases.

What would you say if you wanted to ask permission to take spirit's picture? That would depend on when they lived. You might ask if you could take a snapshot, a photograph, a daguerreotype, or capture a likeness of their image, you most likely would not ask them to sit and take a "selfie" with you unless they had died in the last 5 years or so.

It is also good to remember the lesson we learned on researching the town history and land deeds. If we go back to the example I used of the Winder, Georgia investigation, I would not ask any spirit that died before 1894 anything about "Winder", I would refer to it as Snodon, The Jug, or Jug Tavern because "Winder" would not mean anything to them.

The more you now about how to communicate, the better results you are possibly going to have. It is knowledge that is good to have in the back of your mind because you never know what era you will be visiting when you chat with the spirit interested in communicating with you.

We have gone over several different things you can research before even turning on the first piece of equipment. I hope that you have learned some new ideas to incorporate into your research. Even if you are one of those groups that do their research post investigation, all the information and resources I have given you will work for that as well. Having this knowledge can help you do a more thorough investigation and just might give you interesting things to include in your report to the client. When we do our reveal, I always include a copy of all the research I did with the case report. It makes you look more professional, and it lets them know you actually care about their case.

Can you do this for every investigation you go on? You might not be able to find all the different kinds of resources for a location, but everyone can know the correct phrases to use, the right and respectful way to interact with who you encounter and the history of the era they lived.

Put yourself in their shoes; would you be more inclined to talk with someone who addressed you the proper way, seemed to care about your plight, and might even know your parents, spouse, or child's name, or with someone that just showed up and said, "Yo dude, so how did you croak?"

Paranormal investigation is about gathering information/data respectfully, and thorough pre-investigation research is a great way to show that you respect not only the client but also the spirit and what they may have endured as well.

Permissions

At one time or another, you have probably heard someone say a variant of, "We are going to go check out this old abandoned house, it looks like it would be haunted and nobody owns it, do you want to come with us." There is no land in the United States that is unowned. Just because it has an abandoned structure, does not mean it does not belong to someone. Whether it is a person, business, bank, or government authority, that land is owned and you will be trespassing if you do not receive permission to be there.

In the state of Georgia, where we live, the statue reads:

Georgia Code - Crimes and Offenses - Title 16, Section 16-7-21

(a) A person commits the offense of criminal trespass when he or she intentionally damages any property of another without consent of that other person and the damage thereto is $500.00 or less or knowingly and maliciously interferes with the possession or use of the property of another person without consent of that person.

(b) A person commits the offense of criminal trespass when he or she knowingly and without authority:

(1) Enters upon the land or premises of another person or into any part of any vehicle, railroad car, aircraft, or watercraft of another person for an unlawful purpose;

(2) Enters upon the land or premises of another person or into any part of any vehicle, railroad car, aircraft, or watercraft of another person after receiving, prior to such entry, notice from the owner, rightful occupant, or, upon proper identification, an authorized representative of the owner or rightful occupant that such entry is forbidden; or

(3) Remains upon the land or premises of another person or within the vehicle, railroad car, aircraft, or watercraft of another person after receiving notice from the owner, rightful occupant, or, upon proper identification, an authorized representative of the owner or rightful occupant to depart.

(c) For the purposes of subsection (b) of this Code section, permission to enter or invitation to enter given by a minor who is or is not present on or in the property of the minor's parent or guardian is not sufficient to allow lawful entry of another person upon the land, premises, vehicle, railroad car, aircraft, or watercraft owned or rightfully occupied by such minor's parent or guardian if such parent or guardian has previously given notice that such entry is forbidden or notice to depart.

(d) A person who commits the offense of criminal trespass shall be guilty of a misdemeanor.

(e) A person commits the offense of criminal trespass when he or she intentionally defaces, mutilates, or defiles any grave marker, monument, or memorial to one or more deceased persons who served in the military service of this state, the United States of America or any of the states thereof, or the Confederate States of America or any of the states thereof, or a monument, plaque, marker, or memorial which is dedicated to, honors, or recounts the military service of any past or present military personnel of this state, the United States of America or any of the states thereof, or the Confederate States of America or any of the states

thereof if such grave marker, monument, memorial, plaque, or marker is privately owned or located on land which is privately owned.

In Georgia, a private property owner does NOT have to have "no trespassing" signs posted. If you step foot on their land without permission and cause any kind of damage you are guilty of criminal trespass (a misdemeanor) and can be prosecuted in a court of law. The dollar amount of the damage can change it from a misdemeanor to a felony.

All state's statutes vary so make sure you read the applicable rules for where you are or better yet, just do not trespass. It will save you from a criminal record or possible death via an angry owner's shotgun.

If the property owner or agent is not going to be present during the time you are there, it is best to get them to sign a form stating you have permission to be there. Be sure to note that a minor cannot give permission.

If you are investigating a business or non-occupied historical property, it is also best to let the local authorities know that you will be there if possible. It will save you the headache of being interrupted during a critical time of the investigation to prove you are allowed to be there.

Pre-made permission and confidentiality forms are always a good thing to have on hand. The appendix shows an example of what we use.

Safety

When you hear the word "safety" in regards to investigating, you are probably thinking, YES, I have a first aid kit (at least I hope you do), but in reality "safety" encompasses so much more than that. The location you are investigating can dictate the kind of dangers you might face, but let us get the boring stuff out of the way first. Below are the items recommended for you standard first aid kit:

- Watertight container to hold everything
- First aid manual
- Non-latex gloves
- Disposable N95 masks
- Assorted sizes of band aids (including blister pads)
- Assorted sizes of gauze bandages
- Bandage tape
- Roller gauze
- Triangular bandages
- Antibiotic ointment
- Antiseptic wipes
- Hydrocortisone
- Sterile water
- Alcohol wipes
- Allergy medication
- Pain reliever medications
- Cold and hot packs
- Tweezers
- Sewing kit
- Safety pins
- Scissors
- Hand sanitizer
- Bug spray
- Sunscreen
- Lighter
- Cotton swabs

If any of your team members require something special for themselves (inhaler, allergy injector pen etc.) make sure those items are on your equipment checklist and that they have them when they arrive. It is a very good idea to have at least two people on your team trained in CPR and first aid. I recommend two in case one of the people trained is the person requiring assistance. If you have diabetics on your team, make sure you keep a snack kit that includes things that have carbohydrates or that there is fruit juice available. Investigations can sometimes be stressful, and as a diabetic myself, I know stress can affect my blood sugar.

Let's face it, you're spending time wandering around in the dark, so anyone can get bumps, cuts or scrapes on an investigation. Those are easy to notice immediately and to take care of at the time they happen. There are many things people do not think about though. Asbestos, mold, stinging insects, rusty nails, ticks, snakes, and rodents are things that are not always on your mind. ALL of these can be deadly, so you need to be knowledgeable about them and be prepared.

Asbestos

What is it?
Asbestos is a naturally occurring fibrous material that was a popular as a building material because of its tensile strength, fire protection properties, and chemical resistance. Its use was widespread in many industries even prior to the 20th century. In the 1970s, the federal government started placing bans on how it

could be utilized because of the illnesses that were being linked to it.

Where can it be found?

- Attic and wall insulation produced containing vermiculite
- Vinyl floor tiles and the backing on vinyl sheet flooring and adhesives
- Roofing and siding shingles
- Textured paint and patching compounds used on wall and ceilings
- Walls and floors around wood-burning stoves protected with asbestos paper, millboard, or cement sheets
- Hot water and steam pipes coated with asbestos material or covered with an asbestos blanket or tape
- Oil and coal furnaces and door gaskets with asbestos insulation
- Heat-resistant fabrics
- Automobile clutches and brakes

How can you be exposed?

In general, exposure may occur only when the asbestos-containing material is disturbed or damaged in some way to release particles and fibers into the air. The greater the exposure to asbestos, the greater the chance of developing harmful health effects.

Sign and Symptoms

Sign and symptoms can include but are not limited to:

- Shortness of breath, wheezing, or hoarseness
- A persistent cough that gets worse over time
- Blood in sputum
- Pain or tightening in the chest
- Difficulty swallowing
- Swelling of the neck or face
- Loss of appetite
- Weight loss
- Fatigue or anemia

Effects from exposure

Asbestos-related conditions can be difficult to identify. Healthcare providers usually identify the possibility of asbestos exposure and related health conditions like lung disease by taking a thorough medical history. This includes looking at the person's medical, work, cultural and environmental history. After a doctor suspects an asbestos-related health condition, he or she can use a number of tools to help make the actual diagnosis. Some of these tools are physical examination, chest x-ray, and pulmonary function tests. Your doctor may also refer you to a specialist who treats diseases caused by asbestos.

The possible diseases are:

- Lung Cancer
- Mesothelioma
- Asbestosis (a type of pneumoconiosis)

How to protect against it:
Investigators should wear National Institute for Occupational Safety and Health (NIOSH) approved respirators that fit properly when asbestos disturbance may occur.

Mold

What is it?
Mold is a moisture-loving fungus made up of spores of various sizes. Some mold spores are as small as 3 microns, while others are as large as 40 microns. Mold spores also vary in color. For instance, mold spores that grow behind wallpaper often have a yellow or pink hue. Mold spores that grow on open walls and tile are usually green, brown and sometimes black. Black mold is often the most worrisome.

While the presence of regular mold is not ideal, the existence of black or toxic mold poses serious health risks. Regular mold becomes dangerous when it begins to produce toxins. The poisonous toxin associated with black mold is mycotoxin. Mycotoxins are organic compounds or secondary metabolites that play no direct role in the growth of the mold. It is also important to note that mycotoxins are not only associated with indoor molds but plant crops as well.

(photo courtesy of Dawn Jones)

Where can it be found?
- Indoors: anywhere there are high humidity levels
- Outdoors: damp and shady areas where there is decomposition taking place

How can you be exposed?
Most, if not all, exposures come from touching or inhaling the mold spores.

Signs and Symptoms
- Sneezing
- Nasal and sinus congestion
- Cough
- Runny nose
- Itchy, red, watery eyes
- Wheezing
- Difficulty breathing
- Throat irritation
- Chest tightness

Effects from Mold Exposure
Molds and other fungi may adversely affect human health through allergies, infections, or toxicity. Outdoor molds are generally more abundant than indoor molds. Allergic responses are most commonly experienced as allergic asthma or hay fever. A rare, but much more serious immune-related condition, hypersensitivity pneumonitis (HP), may follow exposure to very high concentrations of fungal molds. Most fungi generally are not pathogenic to healthy humans but can infect immune compromised people (cancer, HIV, diabetics etc.) more easily. I am diabetic and have had fungal pneumonia and it is no fun to get rid of.

Lead Poisoning

What is it?
Lead poisoning is a serious and sometimes fatal condition. It can be found in lead-based paints, including paint on the walls of old houses, buildings, and on toys. Lead poisoning occurs when lead is ingested. It can also be caused by breathing in dust that contains lead. You cannot smell or taste lead and it is not visible to the naked eye. In the United States, lead was a common additive in paint and gasoline. Although these products are no longer produced with lead, lead is still present everywhere, especially in older homes and buildings.

A few common sources of lead include:
- House paint prior to 1978
- Toys made and painted outside the US
- Toys and household items painted before 1978
- Bullets, curtain weights and fishing sinkers
- Pipes and sink faucets
- Jewelry, pottery and lead figures

Signs of repeated exposure include:
- Abdominal pain and/or cramps
- Aggressive behavior
- Sleep problems
- Constipation
- Irritability
- Headaches
- Loss of appetite
- Fatigue
- High blood pressure
- Memory loss
- Numbness or tingling in extremities
- Kidney dysfunction
- Anemia
- Muscle weakness
- Vomiting
- Seizures
- Coma

Lead poisoning is diagnosed through a blood lead test. This test is performed on a standard blood sample. Additional tests may include blood tests to look at the amount of iron storing cells in the blood, x-rays, and possibly a bone marrow biopsy. If you think you have been exposed during an investigation, seek medical attention from your primary doctor.

Other Hazards

Attics and basements can contain several kinds of hazards besides asbestos, mold, and lead. Stinging insects love to make their nests in attics (as do bats, mice, rats and squirrels) and they do not particularly like being disturbed, so make sure any team members that have allergies have their allergy injection pens. It is also common to run into nails that have not been driven through wood properly, so it is a good idea for everyone to be up to date on their tetanus shots.

Broken bones or death from serious head injury is not your objective when investigating. When you are at older locations (and sometimes even newer ones), there are many different hazards you need to be aware of. Loose stairs and floorboards can cause life-threatening injuries if you are not paying attention. It is not always possible to see that you are about to step on a rotten area while you are in the attic and that your butt is about to be one or more floors down very quickly. You will not always be able to tell a step is loose and will catapult you to the bottom, so keep a watchful eye where you are stepping.

Always make sure to check the outside areas during daylight so that you can make note of any obstacles that you may not see if you have to be in that area in the dark. It is always good to know your exits, no matter where you are or what you are doing. When you are investigating, it is especially important since you never know what kind of situation will necessitate a quick departure.

Outdoor Hazards

Outdoor investigations can carry their own hazards. Most people will think about snakes and stinging insects when outside, but forget about ticks. If you are going to be outside in ANY kind of wooded area, make sure you have hats or scarves for your head, long pants, and bug spray. It is a good idea to find a detailed tick identification chart online and print out a copy for you to have on hand. Lyme disease is no joke and can lead to death, but it is only one illness you need to worry about. There are approximately 14 different tick borne diseases that affect humans, so research the area you will be at to see what kinds of ticks you might encounter. In 2016, we were called in to investigate a place that had their own unique tick and disease, so it is important to research them.

Use repellents that contain 20 to 30% DEET on exposed skin and clothing such as boots, socks, and pants according to the label directions, making careful note on the kinds of materials that can be treated safely. Treat gear like packs, sleeping bags, and tents. Bathe or shower as soon as possible after coming indoors. This will wash off any ticks crawling on you and help find any that may have attached. Conduct a full body check with a hand mirror or full length wall mirror or have someone you trust check you for ticks in areas you cannot see. Check clothing and gear. Ticks can hitch a ride on these things and attach to you later. Tumble clothing that is safe to be put in the dryer on high heat for 30 minutes to an hour to kill any ticks hiding in the cloth.

Spiritual Safety

Now that you know about some physical safety hazards, let us talk about the spiritual ones.

It is a good idea to arm yourself with spiritual protection to ward off the influences and effects of negative or demonic activity. What kind of protection you use is your own personal choice. Many people will wear or carry crosses, St. Michael medallions or various types of crystals believed to have protection properties. Teams or individuals may have certain prayers they say both before and after an investigation. Some of the most hard nosed skeptics can become believers the instant they have an encounter or something follows them home from an investigation, so it's better to be safe than sorry.

Keeping Your Clients Safe

Clients also need to feel safe with what you are doing as well. There have been accounts of teams, new and well established, that have gone into an investigation with the wrong frame of mind or investigative tactics that actually made the home worse for the clients to live in. When going into a new place to investigate, look at it the same as you would going into a person's house you have just met for some type of social gathering. You are not going to just walk in and start shouting and demanding things, you are more than likely going to be very respectful. Talk to the spirits as you would a new friend, or better yet someone's grandparents, and you will be doing two things at once. One, you will be opening a healthy line of communication and two you will not be stirring up things and making the atmosphere worse for your client. The things we say and do can and will have an impact on the location after you leave.

Some clients will feel better if you can offer references, especially historic properties, or they may require them. Do not be offended if they ask for them, too many places have been burned (literally) and want to know the people they are letting on their property are trustworthy. It is a good idea to have a combination of residential, business, and historical references, but make sure these clients AGREE to be a reference before you give out their contact information. Another good idea, if it is affordable in your jurisdiction, is to have background checks done on your members and provide a copy to the client or, if you are known (in a good way) to local law enforcement, have them write a good citizen letter.

Lastly, I would like to address something that makes many people nervous. Know the safety of the area you are going to. It is a good idea to check crime reports from the local newspaper or city websites and to check the sex offender list before committing to an investigation. If you do not feel safe going to that area, do not go. More likely than not, you will be going somewhere and entering a home with residents you are not at all familiar with. It is better to turn down that opportunity than to put yourself at risk. No paranormal encounter is worth the personal harm that potentially awaits you. If you are not sure, drive through the area during the daytime and you will probably get a good sense as to whether it is somewhere you want to be when the sun goes down. If you are a person that owns a firearm, be sure to check the local ordinances for open and concealed carry and for goodness sake do not have it out in the open around the client unless you know their stance on firearms on their property. While the government may say you can have it where you are, many people are scared of them and some businesses have strict policies banning any kind of firearm/weapon.

The Normal Paranormal

Even if you are a believer in ghosts, spirits, spooks, and demons, you should approach every investigation as a skeptic; that while you may personally believe in ghosts, you do not believe every location you go to is haunted. I refer to myself as a "skepiliever." It is understandable that a person might have had a true paranormal experience, but when that happens, sometimes they start to see everything happening around them as paranormal and they may not always understand, or they lose sight of real world situations that could cause what they are experiencing.

Take the claims of occurrences and always try to find the "normal" explanation first. Far too many normal occurrences can appear paranormal. By looking for these, you can really put some client fears to rest because in reality, many people would rather know they just have to fix something in their home versus dealing with the unpredictable "unseen."

Once you have discounted the normal, THEN you can proceed with a paranormal investigation.

When you have completed your in-person client interview at the location, you can take your notes and go over those areas looking for non-spook reasons they could occur. You will want to look at things like:

- Electrical (faulty switches, improper grounding, circuit overload, unshielded wiring)
- HVAC (duct work, vents, noises the heat and air make when they kick on, changes in air pressure)
- Plumbing (water hammer, knocking, old valves, leaky toilets, loose faucets)

- Construction (uneven surfaces, creaky floors and steps, door frames, cabinet doors, expansion and contraction)
- Animals (pets and rodents)
- Phantom smells (animal or pest issues, outside smells, cooking smells, smells on clothing, air fresheners near heating/air vents, mold)
- Environmental contamination (EMF, air traffic, automobile traffic, trains, warning sirens, close neighbors)

Every single one of those things above **AND MORE** can cause people to think they have ghosts when they do not. All it takes is the right kind of wind suction when a door is opened in some part of the house to make another one slam shut. Are doors opening and closing a room with a fireplace? Do you know that wind traveling across the top of the chimney outside can reduce the air pressure in the room the fireplace is in and open or close a door? Are the doors misbehaving in the room when a fire is going in the fireplace? The updraft can cause the same issue as the wind outside.

Water hammer is a very real thing in homes. It can sound like a loud thump that shakes the house, or a series of banging noises that happens when the pressure in the water pipe is changed. It can sound like you have the most evil demon imaginable, especially when you are woken up by it in the middle of the night because your icemaker filled up.

Every location is different and will have its own quirks that seem "spooky" to other people but in reality are perfectly normal.

Improper grounding or faulty circuits can cause a host of electrical issues, such as light bulbs exploding or breakers switching off. Unshielded wiring can cause electromagnetic field (EMF) issues that can affect your equipment and your health. These problems are detailed in the equipment section.

Smells are also a big one that can be debunked, especially in homes with animals. Find out if the neighbors are master grillers; people are always amazed at how far smell can travel. Sewage issues are well known to be the cause of that "rotten" smell in someone's basement and air fresheners in any vicinity of an air vent are famous for smelling like "a dear departed grandmother's perfume."

The construction of a house can also cause big issues. Anything from floors and doors that are not level to that creaky spot on your stairs can make someone think their house is haunted. Older homes especially can have such severe leveling problems that the floor creates a "funhouse" effect, so that when you walk over them you feel off balance and dizzy. Many stairs have that one spot, and even a cat or dog walking over it can set it off. Your client may tell you that they were laying in the bed when they heard someone on the stairs or walking down the hall and they were the only person in the house, but they often forget their own pets could be causing this noise. Have you ever heard a cat going through its "psycho" time at 2 a.m.? In a house with hardwoods, it can sound like a herd of cattle in your hallway. We sleep with a floor fan running and I can still hear the cats coming down the hall in the middle of the night!

A few good things to have in your investigation kit are a level, to check floors and doors; string or ribbon to check for drafts; a voltmeter to check electrical outlets; colored water flavoring or food coloring that you can use in the toilet tank to check for leaks.

Once you have checked all of these things out, then you can proceed to pull out the rest of your equipment and initiate the next steps in your investigation.

Equipment

You and your team members will probably spend some serious money on equipment to use during your investigations. It is a good idea to have a checklist of what you are taking with you so that you remember to pack it all up after the investigation is over. It should include the name of the equipment and who was in charge of it for the investigation.

Photography/Video

There are many makes and models of still photography and video equipment that can be used on an investigation. The thing to keep in mind is that no matter how much you do or do not spend, real visual evidence is rare. It is going to depend on several factors like:

- the lighting
- the amount of dust, bugs and moisture in the area
- the spectrum you are shooting in
- your knowledge of how your camera works (exposures and shutter speed)
- keeping objects like camera straps, fingers, hair, breath and smoke out of the way
- just plain luck.

Not only do you need to keep all this in mind when you do your evidence review, but you need to remember that pareidolia, or matrixing, is a very real thing.

Pareidolia is a psychological phenomenon involving a stimulus (an image or a sound) where the mind perceives a familiar pattern of something where none actually exists. **note that it includes sound**

I cannot emphasize this enough: READ the manual that comes with your photography/video equipment. Read it and then read it again. These days orbs (or circles of confusion as some refer to them) are so common, a lot manufacturers are including why you get them in the manuals. Orbs may be produced using a film camera if you wanted them but they are not as prevalent as with digital because of the sensor size.

The internet is full of people talking about orbs and their meanings (especially if they have color to them). When I am not on my soapbox about them, I always say I am coming back as a plaid orb. Those of us that point out what they really are, are often times called haters, bullies and skeptics. This is far from the truth; we just know how a camera works. Here are some examples (unfortunately, they have to be in black and white) of how your camera can make things "appear" to be paranormal, but are not:

(photo courtesy of Dawn Jones)

Camera Strap

Hair

Hair

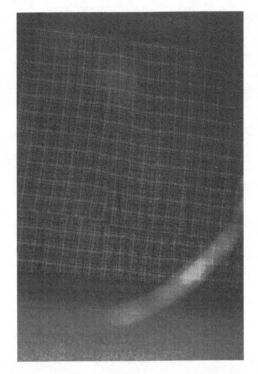

Hair

Incorrect Shutter Speed

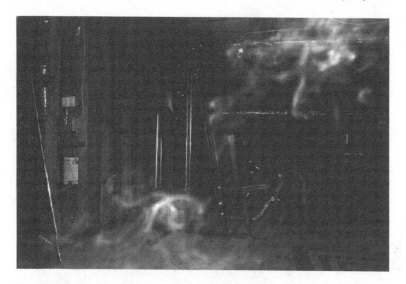

(photo courtesy of Dawn Jones)

Smoke

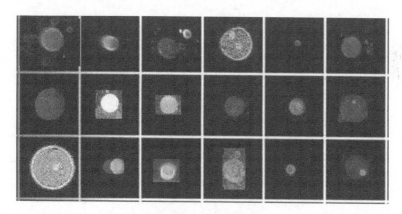

Dust Orb Examples

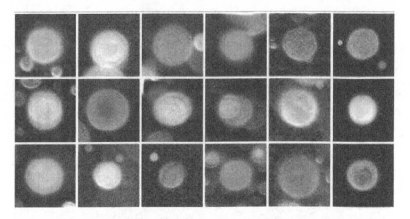

Moisture Orb Examples

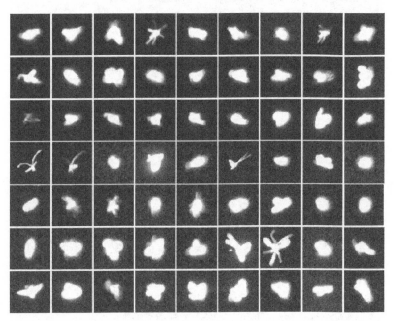

Insect Examples

You would be best served by taking the camera equipment you have and experimenting with how the things shown above look on YOUR equipment.

Audio

Although a parapsychologist by the name of Konstantin Raudive popularized the idea of EVPs in the 1970s, people were trying to record them even earlier than that. Attila Szalay started experimenting in the 1940s using a 78-rpm record and switched to reel-to-reel machines in the 1950s. Skeptics tell us that it is an audio form of auditory pareidolia or apophenia, but people that have heard very relevant answers to questions they have asked will wildly disagree. Electronic voice phenomena (EVP) are not heard with the human ear at the time of the occurrence and they fall into three categories:

Classification A EVP: A clear and distinct voice or sound that is accepted and not disputed because it is understood by anyone with normal hearing and they can understand it without being told what another person hears. You can normally hear a Class A without the use of headphones.

Classification B EVP: A voice or sound that is somewhat loud and distinct. B Class is more common and many people can hear it after being told what to listen for. It is usually audible to experienced persons who have learned the skill of listening to EVP. It can sometimes be heard without the use of headphones.

Classification C EVP: A faint voice or sound that can barely be heard. It is sometimes indecipherable and unintelligible. It may have paranormal characteristics, such as a mechanical sound. Most investigators would apply objectivity and disregard it, but may save it for reference purposes.

Some teams only use their voice recorders in what are called "burst" sessions. In my opinion, this does your investigation a disservice. We have captured some of the best EVP while a conversation during an investigation break is going on. While your evidence reviewer might not like it, keeping your recorder running from start to finish is a brilliant idea because you never know when someone unseen might want to voice an opinion about your discussion.

Audible Voice Phenomena (AVP) are disembodied voices heard by the investigator at the time of occurrence; they may or may not be picked up by recording devices. Some of my biggest disappointments during evidence review have been when we heard something with our own ears, remark about it, but then you cannot hear it on the recorder during playback.

When doing your evidence review, it is always a good idea to play your suspected AVP/EVP for another person without telling him or her what you are hearing. If the two of you differ on what the word or phrase is, it is best to throw it out. We will not present anything but a Class A EVP to our clients as "evidence".

Spirit Boxes

Both Konstantin Raudive and Friedrich Jürgenson were the early pioneers of today's spirit boxes (a device used for contacting spirits through radio frequency). Experiments were conducted in an RF shielded laboratory (remember this part, it will be important) where voices were recorded as coming through radios.

People started experimenting with this the 1940s. It was said if you tuned a radio to a place on the dial where no radio was coming through, you could have a two way, immediate conversation with the dead. It was the earliest form of Instrumental Trans-Communication (ITC), a phrase made popular in the 1970s.

People mistakenly believe Frank Sumption invented the first "ghost box" in 2002, but in actuality, the first attempt was in 1980 by a man named William O'Neil.

Spiricom

He built the Spiricom based on the instructions of George Mueller, a man that had been deceased for 6 years. George was known to frequently communicate with several ITC researchers at the time, even via telephone.

Frank's ghost box eventually evolved into the version we have today of the PSB-7 and 11 made by Gary

Frank's Box

Galka, after his daughter was killed in a car crash, and in his attempt to communicate with her.

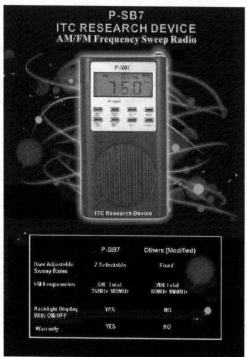

Gary Galka's PSB-7

Skeptic attitudes aside, there is one big problem with spirit boxes. People are not using them correctly, and the fault lies both on the internet and TV shows. The point of a spirit box is for the spirit to communicate in their own voice, through the white noise that is generated. This is why researchers were getting such good results experimenting with the different bands on radios. It did not involve "sweeping." These days you will see people using a spirit box with the antenna extended and an external speaker with Bluetooth capability on the slowest sweep because they mistakenly believe that the spirit is using the bits of radio bleed to communicate. This is not how they are supposed to work. Others read that people on ghost shows have removed the antenna and crack theirs open to do the same thing. That will help kill the radio bleed… until you plug in an external speaker. The wire from the speaker to the spirit box creates a new antenna, voiding all the "work" you just did to remove it. Have you ever noticed that when they are used on TV you NEVER hear radio bleed, no matter where they are walking around with it? I can understand that, if they are in some kind of bunker or underground, but it seems mighty fishy to me that when they are in a city, you never hear anything other than the "spirit response".

Remember earlier when I said to remember Konstantin, a pioneer in ITC, conducted his experiments in an RF shielded room? There was a reason for that. YOU DO NOT WANT THE RADIO COMING THROUGH. If you are going to use a spirit box, you need to shield it from radio frequency, but you do not want to shield it so much the spirits cannot use it. "Ghost hunter" stores sell an item called a faraday bag. This is a waste of money; that thing is so strong it will kill all reception to things like your cellphone.

The easiest way we have found to RF shield your spirit box enough to kill the radio (most of it anyway), but still allow the spirit to come through in their own voice is to place it (with or without a speaker) in a computer static zip lock bag. If you are investigating near a city like Atlanta, you may need two bags inside each other to kill off most of the reception.

If you experiment with this, you will be amazed at the difference in the results you do/don't get. If you are interested in the history of ITC, this documentary is a must see, you can google "ITC Calling Earth" to find this link: https://vimeo.com/101171248.

Electromagnetic Field (EMF)

What is EMF? What produces EMF? Why do we care about EMF? Do you know that your "ghost hunting" EMF detector is probably not doing what you think it is?

Electric fields are created by differences in voltage; the higher the voltage, the stronger the field. They are measured in V/m. Magnetic fields are created when electric current flows and are measured in milligauss (mG) or nano tesla (nT); the greater the current, the stronger the magnetic field. An electric field will exist even when there is no current flowing. If current does flow, the strength of the magnetic field will vary with power consumption but the electric field strength will be constant.

Electromagnetic fields are present everywhere. They can be both natural and manmade. Did you know that the human body produces EMF?

Paranormal investigators use things such as the Mel Meter, Tri-field Meter, K2, and in the old days, Geiger counters, and compasses to try to see if a spirit is present and/or communicating with you. The thought process behind it is that a spirit emits energy when they are present, energy that was not registering before their arrival. It is up to you to decide whether you believe this is a valid form of communication before asking them to make the pretty lights come on and off, but there are some things you need to keep in mind when it comes to EMF. Constant sources of high EMF are dangerous and detrimental to your health and well-being. It can even produce what is referred to by some as magnetic hallucinations.

How NOT to be a Ghost Hunter

There is a dispute in the community about "EMF Sickness" and just how harmful it is. Personally, I can tell you that when I am in an area with high EMF, I suffer symptoms that completely go away when I leave the area, so I do not dispute it at all. If you are sensitive to EMF, you can experience.

- Headaches
- Heart palpitations
- Skin burning or tingling
- Rashes
- Sleep problems
- Ringing in the ears
- Fatigue, no matter how much sleep you get
- Brain fog
- Anxiety
- Problems with your immune system
- Vertigo
- Nausea
- Mood swings
- Twitching of limbs
- Depression

Here is a good example of how EMF can be mistaken for "ghosts" (and this happens more often than not):

A client was complaining of seeing dark figures in his bedroom, experiencing horrific nightmares, migraine headaches, nausea, and sleepwalking. These things did not happen anywhere else at any time and gave us our first clue it was not a ghost.

"Normal" EMF readings are going to be anywhere from .01 to .06 milligauss depending on what is emitting it. When we arrived at the client's home, the first thing we did was go to the bedroom with our meter and measure what the alarm clock beside his bed was reading. It registered as 60, not a .60, but 60.00. When we pulled the meter out to see where it dissipated, it was still a 30 at his pillow. That is a high constant barrage of EMF, which could cause all of his symptoms. We had him move his clock away from the bed and his "ghost" problems disappeared.

EMF can be the cause of so many medical problems, it is important to rule it out for a client before you do anything else. Since some studies link long-term EMF exposure to things such as Cushing's syndrome, adrenal tumors and various kinds of cancer, you could just be saving their life.

When you are using your EMF meter, unless you have paid a hefty sum for it, it is most like one you got for "ghost hunting." You need to keep in mind that the meters sold specifically for hunting that "wascally ghost" are only a single axis meter. That means every time you move it, you are measuring a different angle of the field. Because of that, it is not a good idea to walk around with your meter during an investigation; keep it stationary. If you have it near anything made of steel, the slightest vibration can register a change in the mG. Let's say you have it near a set of filing cabinets that vibrate with traffic outside. If a heavy truck or train goes by making them vibrate enough, you will see a change on the EMF meter. Also, keep in mind that anything that has relays, transformers, capacitors, or switches can make it register a change.

While we are talking about EMF meters, let me share with you an experience we had that embarrassed me at first, but I later realized was a great teaching example.

How NOT to be a Ghost Hunter

Since David and I are just a two-person team, we seldom have a need for walkie-talkies. We have them, but rarely use them and until recently, we had never actually had them on during an investigation.

Keep in mind as you read this, you're going to see exactly what was happening, but this is one of those good "in the heat of the moment" things that happened and even as seasoned as I am, I didn't see it until later. It just goes to show that we can always learn something.

We were doing a fundraiser investigation at a state park, and there were so many people in attendance, we thought it best to split the group up with me leading one, and David leading the other, resulting in us getting the walkies out.

The plan was for the groups to switch after a certain period of time so that they each had time with both of us. We had let members of the group use our equipment so they could see what it was like. When it came time to switch I just had them leave their piece of equipment on so I did not have to mess with turning them all off and back on again with the new group. They left the structure we were at and I keyed the mic on the walkie-talkie to let David know they were headed his way. We were talking back and forth when I noticed the proximity meter on my EMF detector that was sitting stationary on the floor was going off. We have had this thing for years, it had NEVER gone off on its own, and it just kept doing it repeatedly.

I will admit I got extremely excited and started saying my normal phrase ("holy crap") that I say when something unexpected happens. I am yelling at David thru the walkie that it is just repeatedly going off while

I grab one of the video recorders to film the whole thing. I was literally so excited I was hopping up and down. My new group comes into the cabin we are in and I noticed it stopped, and I was really disappointed they wouldn't be able to see and excitedly explaining to them what had happened. It never went off again that night.

The next morning I was downloading and clipping the video from the camera so I could show David what happened. That is when it hit me. The proximity meter went of every single time I keyed the mic on the walkie-talkie and I was dumbfounded. I would expect it to register a change on a K2, but not this. I was wrong.

I started messaging my friends that I knew had different kinds of proximity meters and used walkie-talkies to ask them if they had ever noticed this, only one had. Jeffery very kindly set up his video camera to show me how the walkies affected various pieces of his equipment (motion sensors, EMF meters with the proximity meter and stand-alone proximity meters) and I spent the rest of the day feeling REALLY stupid. But, like I said, once I had time to think about it, I was really glad it had happened because now I had something else I could pass along to people that may not realize it and prove that even I can get swept up in the moment.

Miscellaneous

Who uses an IR thermometer as opposed to an ambient thermometer during an investigation? I know many people do and they even sell them at the hunting stores. Put.It.Away. Seriously, stop using it. IR thermometers do not measure ambient temperature; they do not find "cold or hot" spots. They measure black body radiation emitted from the object the laser is aimed at and that will do you no good during an investigation.

How many of you know how to use and store your batteries properly? If you do, then I am guessing that always exciting and expletive producing battery drain is not a problem for you. It is possible to buy batteries that are no good. It is possible that you are not storing them correctly and they are being affected by temperature. It is possible that you are using rechargeable batteries and not recharging them according to the manufacturer's suggestions. I do not recommend rechargeable batteries, but if you are going to use them, use them on something besides an investigation to see how much life you get out of them and always make sure to recharge them the way the maker says to. For regular batteries, I suggest having a battery checker that you can use to check them all before you start your investigation. If you do that, you might just notice that your battery drain problem happens less frequently.

UV flashlights are a great thing to use, especially when you have phantom smells. They can show you places animals or rodents have left their mark that are invisible to the naked eye. Another thing to note is that when you use a regular flashlight, you always want to use one with a red filter. This will help your eyes not have to readjust to their natural night vision when you turn it on.

Do you remember to cut off the air conditioner or furnace when you start your investigation? I have been dumbfounded on investigations we have done with other teams that leave them running and do not take into account temperature changes that may be the result of being too close to a vent.

Trigger objects are items you can use during your investigation. The theory behind them is that they mean something to the spirit and might evoke a response from them. They can be fun to experiment with, especially if you have done your pre-investigation research and have some idea what the situation might be. You can use music, toys, interactive objects etc. the list could go on forever. Birthday candles are always interesting. If one of your team is having a birthday, or if it might be near the birthday of the supposed spirit, bringing along a small cupcake and a birthday candle could possibly bring about great results. In the end, just remember, your most important piece of equipment is yourself and your six senses. Sometimes the best "evidence" will not be recordable, but a personal experience.

Paranormal Investigation

Once you have ruled out the possibility of normal occurrences making your client believe they are being visited by the demon from hell, you can turn off your cell phones *gasp*, go about your investigation, and wait for the spirit to go through its own check list.

GHOST TO DO LIST

1. Move something
2. Talk into the red light
3. Turn on the flashlight
4. End "shave & a haircut"
5. Make all the lights light up
6. Appear as an orb
7. Touch someone or pull their hair
8. Slam a door
9. Say someone's name
10. Make the numbers on the EMF meter change
11. Knock on a wall
12. Shout GET OUT
13. Show myself

Timeless Paranormal

Cell Phones

Cell phones as an investigation tool are generally not a good idea. It does not matter that you paid for the latest ghost hunting app, or that it has a voice recorder, compass or camera. Cell phone technology is RF based therefore, it will affect your other equipment. It is a bad idea to have them powered on when investigating. Even when it is in airplane mode it is still reading RF signals and can make your meters and spirit boxes give results that are NOT evidence. There is ONE time we advocate using your cell phone and that is if you have invested in the Flir One.

Since most of us fund our investigations from left over grocery money, the Flir One is a cool thing to have and ok to use as long as you are not using it while using any other equipment. Just keep in mind, like all other visual equipment, it too, is subject to scrutiny.

Think Outside the Box

Most of the time, you see the client being told they have to leave the premises during an investigation. Let me tell you why some people think that is not such a good idea. If there is paranormal activity going on in the home, that spirit is used to the client being there. They do not know you and it is entirely possible you make them uncomfortable. Imagine that, the ghost being scared of you! That could be one reason why you do not experience the activity that has been reported. By keeping the client there, it might encourage repeat behaviors and it shows the client exactly what you are doing while you are in their home making it a win-win situation for everyone.

Try to be inventive with your investigation. Do not just sit around in the dark asking the same old boring questions. Some teams have noticed that some of their best experiences have been while they were not "actively" investigating. Spirits can be like children, all they want is attention, and they will do anything to get it. Sometimes that is perceived as "bad," "negative", or "demonic" when in reality they just want to be noticed.

If they have enough energy, they can throw things, pull your hair, or scratch your arm (just to name a few). When you give them respectful attention, you are far more likely to get some good results. If you want to do something different, take what you learned about the possible spirit and use that. If you know it was a lady from the 1700s or 1800s, set up your equipment and have a tea party and invite them to join you. Have a birthday party or a slumber party. The options are limitless and a lot more fun than sitting on the floor in the dark waiting to have your heart stop from a startle reflex because someone in the room passed gas.

Here is some food for thought: The majority of investigations you see on TV are done in the dark. The thought behind that is that there is less contamination. The everyday hustle and bustle noise levels are lower giving your audio a better chance of being legitimate; if the spirit is producing its own light, you might miss it if the lights are on, and it is just spookier.

Do not insist on always investigating in the dark, keep some lights on, or do it during the daytime. If you listen to your client, a LOT of the time the things that are happening to them are going on in broad daylight, while they are sitting around watching TV, or having game night with all the lights on. What if your ghost shows up looking like a normal person, not some ethereal Hollywood version? If you are sitting in the dark, you are not going to see them!

Investigation Hangover & Client Aftercare

After the investigation is over, please make sure to leave the place as you found it and then assure the client that you will be getting back in touch with them at a later date whether you have "captured" evidence or not. Be clear that it will probably take a while since thorough evidence review is extremely time consuming, as is writing up the report.

Investigation hangover is a real thing. You have spent days, weeks, or months leading up to the event. You have spent all your energy on getting what you need to have a successful investigation. Dealing with scared clients can be stressful, as is getting prepared. Couple that with staying up past your bedtime and it is a recipe for exhaustion. Way back when, I was eager to start my evidence review right away, but I learned that if you take good notes during and immediately afterwards, it is best to wait several days before diving into review.

Evidence review can be exciting, boring, and a great cure for insomnia. Just think about this: a 4-hour investigation with as little as two audio recorders and two video cameras can yield a minimum of 48 hours in evidence review. You've got at least 16 hours of audio (because you should always listen through it at least twice) and there is no way you can watch the whole video screen, so you have to divide it in quarters, that's 32 hours on that. You are going to be glued to a chair for a long time trying to find two seconds of epic evidence. I cannot tell you the times I have caught myself falling asleep while reviewing video footage and I have to start all over. Limit the amount of reviewing done in one sitting, the chance of catching something that way outweighs what you catch when you try to do it too quickly.

No matter what you think you find in your evidence review, be sure to have someone else look at or listen to it, even the skeptic in your group, if you have one. If there is any dissent on it, throw it out. You do not want to be one of those teams that are mocked for finding "something" at every investigation.

In the end, if you conclude that the claims of activity were true and you believe there to be true paranormal activity, you need to have a plan for the homeowner AND the spirit. Some of these earthbound spirits just want to be on their way; that is why they have been trying to get someone's attention.

If you do not have someone on your team that is able to help the spirit, have a recommendation for the client. Absolutely, positively do not leave the client or spook hanging. One of my biggest pet peeves is a client who wants to keep "their ghost" and does not want someone moving them on. We tell our clients up front that if we find a spirit looking for help, we will provide that for them. I am sad to report that we have missed some investigations because the client was more interested in their location being haunted than in helping a lost soul. The sad part about this endeavor is that you have to respect the boundaries your client sets on whether they want just an investigation or an investigation and help for the spirit.

Earthbound spirits are not pets and every single one should be offered the option of getting help moving on. If they choose not to, it should be their decision, not the clients.

Paranormal investigating is not a recognized "science," it never will be. As you saw in the newspaper headlines, people have been trying to use science to prove the existence of the afterlife for a very long time. You are going to have to be comfortable with the fact that this will never happen. There is just no way to come up with a hypothesis and test your theories because you cannot get the same results every single time you do an investigation, and consistent verifiable results is the basis of science.

There will always be roadblocks along the way. People will tell you that you are wasting your time, or that you are nuts or that you are going to hell for talking to dead people. Just remember why you decided on doing it in the first place.

I hope that your reason is to help.

Bonus Material!

Why Do You Wake Up at the Same Time?

"I always wake up at 2:46 a.m., what does this mean?"

I cannot tell you how many times I have seen a variant of this question. As a long time paranormal researcher and educator, it is my obligation to let you know that it does not mean that the ghost cat of your long dead Aunt Maranda is trying to let you know she is being held captive by a demon. It also probably does not mean you are "gifted" and getting messages from the other side. It does not have anything to do with being around the purported "witching hour." Unless you are being yanked out of bed at that time and dragged down the hall by your hair or you have a garbage truck beep beeping outside your house at that time every day, it more than likely means your body is trying to tell you something.

Pop culture has gone a long way in influencing the way we see things related to the paranormal. More than 300 years ago, people were hung, burned, compressed, and all sorts of ugly things for even a hint that a person might be "gifted." In the 1800's spiritualism gained momentum and the culture of the time made it "cool" to visit mediums and go to séances. Somewhere in the 1900's paranormal phenomena became taboo again, no one wanted to admit their house might be haunted and people scoffed at mediums. Now we are in the 2000's and inundated with paranormal entertainment. Once again, it has become "cool." Mediums and "gifted" people are coming out of the woodwork. I can think of at least four shows on TV right now dedicated to mediums and that does not even include the ghost shows that feature them as part of their investigations.

Now, before you try to burn ME at the stake, do not get me wrong; I do believe ghosts and in mediumship. By very definition, it means someone that communicates with the dead, and isn't that what we as paranormal investigators do? Yes, some of us have an elevated level of that gift and can communicate in ways other than through question and answer sessions using voice recorders and spirit boxes, and we take that ability very seriously because frankly, it can be an awesome and VERY scary experience at the same time.

I digress though. When we do a client interview, a large part of it is dedicated to medical questions. No, we are not being nosy. We do it because those of us that care about our clients do everything in our power to find the normal explanation first, and SO many things can be attributed physiology. The effect of our environment and medical conditions on our body can be amazing if you take the time to seriously look into it.

Adrenal glands are a good example, and one that speaks to the "waking up at the same time every night" problem. Cortisol, produced by the adrenal gland, is normally highest in the morning (6-8am) and then slowly lowers itself throughout the day until it is at its lowest around 11pm – midnight, allowing your body to prepare for sleep. SO many things can affect this, among them, stress, too many carbs during the day, diabetes, and EMF exposure.

EMF is most often talked about as "proof" of ghostly activity, but EMF affects people in ways that is really not talked about enough and it's a real presence in each and every home in the world. Even short-term exposure to EMF can cause you to think you are seeing/hearing ghosts (i.e. hallucinate) and being followed (i.e. paranoia). Long-term exposure is even worse on your body. How many people have you heard say, every time I lay down at night I see faces, hear sounds, get sick to my stomach, feel scared etc.? When we have a client that says that, the very first thing we do is an EMF reading on what is right there beside their bed, and how far out it radiates if we do get a reading. We have seen your normal big box store alarm clocks give off readings as high as 60 at the clock and radiate out to around 30 around the clients pillow. This IS going to affect how you sleep; it is also quite possibly going to affect your long-term health. Fixing this is simple, move the alarm clock to where you are not sleeping in the radius of EMF output (or get a clock that does not need to be plugged in).

That is just one example of something that can cause you to wake up at the same time every night. There is something called the Chinese Medicine Meridian clock (TCM). You can look at this clock, find your "time," and see which organ relates to that time. Phooey you say? Let me give you an example.

I have a specific time I wake up every single night. My time falls between the liver and lung time. It is well known I have ongoing lung issues, but even without that, I am diabetic. Something is tripping my sleep-wake cycle that needs to be corrected; most likely, a spike in my cortisol and adrenalin levels and that something is a drop my blood sugar. Your body increases epinephrine levels when your blood sugar drops too low so it can pull glucose (sugar) from glycogen (stored sugar) from your…wait for it…..LIVER. Your body will increase cortisol to break down valuable anabolic amino acids from protein to convert into glucose to elevate your blood sugar. That surge in either stress hormone will wake me up.

I was diagnosed with type 2 diabetes in 2008 and not long after I started waking up at the exact same time every night. A few months later, we acquired a cat and he would wake me up at the same time I had been waking up on my own every single night (and 8 years later, he still does it). I talked to my doctor about this and she let me know right quick that my sugar was low and that, believe it or not, my cat could tell this and was waking me up to alert me I needed to do something about it. This directly correlates to the TCM.

As you can see, there is a myriad of reasons you are "waking up at the same time." Take a look at the clock, find your time and see which organ falls into that time frame and then do some due diligence research of your own and you might just find that your "demon" is your body trying to tell you something.

If you search for images of the clock online, you can find detailed ones that show which organ corresponds with which time.

Appendix: Client Questionnaire

Use a separate piece of paper if necessary, noting the number and section of the question, if there is not enough room on this form to complete your answer.

I – Personal Information

Full
Name: _____
            Last   **First**   **M.I.**

Address: _____
    Street Address   **Apt./Unit #**

_____
         City   **State**   **Postal Code**

How long have you lived/worked at this location? _____

Home
Phone: ( ) _____ Mobile Phone: _____

E-mail
Address: _____

Location of apparitio n: _____

Dates: _____

II – Witness Information

1 - Full Name: _____ / _____ / _____
                                                   Date of Birth   Sex

2 - Full Name: _____ / _____ / _____
                                                   Date of Birth   Sex

3 - Full Name: _____ / _____ / _____
                                                   Date of Birth   Sex

4 - Full Name: _____ / _____ / _____
                                                   Date of Birth   Sex

III – Encounter Questions

1. Can you describe the paranormal experience?
2. If it was an apparition, how far away was it from the person who reported the sighting?
3. If it was an experience, what happened? What was the person doing when it happened?
4. Did the apparition cast a shadow?
5. Did the entity manipulate make contact with the subject, make sounds, have a smell, or move any objects?
6. Did the entity make eye contact with the subject?
7. Did the entity acknowledge anyone present in any way?
8. Did the entity speak? If so, what exactly did it say?
9. Did the entity move? If yes, explain.
10. Could you see an apparition? If so, was it solid or translucent?
11. What was the apparition wearing?
12. How long was the apparition visible?
13. Was this the first sighting? If not, explain in as much detail as possible (reviewing the questions above).

IV – Conditions at the Time of the Sighting

1. What were the weather conditions like that day?
2. What were the weather conditions at the time of the sighting?
3. Was there any visible lightning?
4. Was thunder heard?
5. Was there any precipitation (rain, snow, hail, fog, mist, etc.)?
6. Were there any electrical problems before, during, or after the sighting?
7. Was there any noticeable variation in the temperature before, during, or after the sighting?

V – Witness Questions

Witness Name: _____ / / _____

                                                Date of   Sex
                                                Birth

1. What were you doing before the experience occurred?
2. What first made you notice the entity's presence?
3. What did you think was happening? If it was an apparition, what did you think it was?
4. Describe what the apparition was doing when you saw it.
5. Did you notice any unusual, or out of place smells, during the experience? If so, please describe the odors.
6. How long did it last, and how did you lose sight of the apparition?
7. Were you sleeping before the experience?
8. Were you feeling tired before the sighting?
9. Describe what you did before, during and after the sighting.
10. Did you attempt to communicate with the entity?
11. Were you able to capture any images of the apparition on film or video?
12. Did you move toward or away from the apparition?
13. Describe your thoughts during the experience:
14. Had you experienced anything like this before?
15. Had anyone you know ever experienced anything similar to this? If so, please describe who, when, and what.

VI – General Questions

1. Were there any animals present at the time?
2. How did the animals act before, during, or after the experience?
3. Did any objects break before, during, or after the experience?
4. Was there any type of physical or sexual attack by the apparition?

5. Did you hear any abnormal sounds? If so, please explain what they sounded like.
6. Did you hear any abnormal voices? If so, what did they sound like, and what was said?
7. Did anything else unusual happen, before during, or after the experience?
8. Have you noticed any patterns of the entity's appearances?
9. Have any shadows been seen?
10. Has anyone felt any cold or hot spots?
11. Has there been a recent death of a loved one?
12. Has there been a recent anniversary of a death, birthday, anniversary, etc.?
13. Has anyone heard any rapping, walking, or knocking?
14. Has anyone experience mood changes in specific rooms or areas of the location?
15. Has anyone had conversations with spirits or entities?
16. Has anyone seen or heard doors opening or closing?
17. Has anyone seen any objects moving or had items disappear?
18. Have there been any electrical/appliance disturbances?
19. Is any resident going through puberty
20. Have there been any recent renovations at the location?
21. Have any noteworthy or intense events happened at the location?
22. Have there been any noticeable patterns to any activity?
23. What could be some possible conventional causes be?
24. Do any of the residents at this location experience unusual mood swings or strange vivid dreams?
25. Do residents become tired, sick, or agitated to an extraordinary extent?
26. Are there any accounts of activity occurring at a previous residence?
27. Is there any history of hoaxes or practical jokes amongst occupants?

V – Investigator Impressions of Occupants

(Note; Do not show to occupants. If they request a copy of the interview, omit this part.)

1. Overall integrity of the occupants: Do the occupants appear sincere in telling their accounts? If not, explain.
2. Does each recounting of the paranormal event remain consistent? If not, explain.
3. Do the occupants agree on the events related to the accounts? If not, explain.
4. Do you believe that any of the occupants would want to perpetuate a hoax for any type of attention? If yes, explain.
5. Do you believe the person(s) being interviewed to be of sound mind (normal rational people)? If yes, explain.
6. Do you believe that there may be any reason to believe that paranormal accounts may be the result of drug use, psychological conditions, overactive imagination, or dishonesty? If yes, explain.
7. Do you believe that further investigation is necessary? If not, explain.

Appendix: Permission & Confidentiality

Permission to Investigate

By filling out the form below, you will allow us to investigate the location in question. All data obtained during the investigation is completely confidential and will never meet the public eye without your written consent. This document also releases you of all liability.

Permission to Investigate

Client Full Name: _____

           Last   **First**   **M.I.**

Address: _____

        Street Address   **Apt./Unit #**

_____

        City   **State**   **Postal Code**

How long have you lived at this location? _____

Home Phone: _____ **Mobile Phone:** _____

E-mail Address: _____

Are you the legal owner: ☐ Yes ☐ No **If not, who is?** _____

Investigator: _____

Contact ( ) _____ **Phone:** _____

I hereby grant permission and allow access to the location identified in this document above for the sole purpose of conducting an investigation into possible paranormal occurrences by a field research team comprised by members of the **Timeless Paranormal**. The investigative team will be allowed to use electrical connections, if available, for the sole purpose of the investigation. The investigator and any individuals accompanying the investigator hereby release the owner and/or property representative (tenant, agent, etc.) from any liability for injuries and/or damages that may occur during the investigation.

The investigators involved and their team assumes responsibility for any damages incurred to the property listed above that was caused directly by the investigative team during the investigation.

The owner and/or property representative also agree to pay for any damages to the investigators equipment provided tampering or sabotage with the equipment by the owner, or any occupant of the property, and/or representative can be verified and documented as being responsible for such damage.

Timeless Paranormal also assumes responsibility for proper releases of information from the property owners as per the signed 'Confidentiality Agreement' form; as no information about the investigation will be released without signed copies of the aforementioned form.

Authorized agent of property: _____   **Date:** ___/___/_____

Printed Name: _____

Investigator Signature: _____   **Date:** ___/___/_____

Printed Name: _____

Confidentiality Agreement

It is understood and agreed to that the below identified discloser of confidential information may provide certain information that is and must be kept confidential. To ensure the protection of such information, and to preserve any confidentiality necessary for peace of mind, it is agreed that:

1. Any information that is designated as 'Confidential' information at the time of this disclosure to the Timeless Paranormal for the investigation at (insert address)

2. The recipient agrees not to disclose the confidential information obtained from the discloser to the public or anyone else unless required to do so by law.

3. The investigation information and/or evidence may be publicly released at the discretion of the Timeless Paranormal with no restriction, if the identity of any witnesses, clients, or location specifics are changed or omitted if desired by the client.
    ☐There is no restriction to location specifics
    ☐Changes and/or omissions to locations specifics must be made (Address kept private)

4. This agreement states the entire agreement between the parties concerning the disclosure of Confidential Information. Any addition or modification to this Agreement must be made in writing and signed by the parties.

5. If any of the provisions of this Agreement are found to be unenforceable, the remainder shall be enforced as fully as possible and the unenforceable

provision(s) shall be deemed modified to the limited extent required to permit enforcement of the Agreement as a whole.

WHEREFORE, the parties acknowledge that they have read and understand this Agreement and voluntarily accept the duties and obligations set forth herein.

Recipient of Confidential Information:

Name
(Print):_____

Signature: _____

Date: _____

Discloser of Confidential Information:

_____

Name (Print):

_____

Signature: _____

Date: _____

About the Author

Shannon lives outside Atlanta, GA with her husband David and her two cats Morgana & Mordred. Her daughter currently resides with her wife in Las Vegas, NV.

She is a genealogist and historian with over 35 years of experience, who frequently helps others with their family research and has worked with multiple historical societies transcribing old documents, research, and grave dowsing. She is a board member of the Wynne-Russell House Preservation Board, an entity that is responsible for the upkeep and promotion of the second oldest home in Gwinnett County, GA. She is also a member of the Gwinnett County Archaeology Society and a board member of the Lilburn Citizens Police Academy Partnership.

Shannon & David joined forces in 2003 and combined two lifetimes of experience in searching for the paranormal. They established Timeless Paranormal in 2013 so that they might have a presence in the paranormal world and gain access to historical locations. In her spare time, what little of it there is, she enjoys reading books authored by her comrades Richard Estep and Kyl T. Cobb, Jr and has a passion for time travel bodice ripping romance and supernatural romance books all while dreaming of finally getting her fiction novel finished. When her schedule allows, you can usually find her at a local sushi place indulging in her addiction to wasabi, but in reality she loves nothing more than snuggling in bed on Friday nights with David watching "spooky" TV aka, whatever paranormal show is on the DVR.